A Passion For Life

To my
good friend
Dean
Best always
Chuck

A Passion For Life

Reflections From The Journey

CHIP WEBSTER

ISBN: 1546781854
ISBN 13: 9781546781851
Library of Congress Control Number: 2017908137
CreateSpace Independent Publishing Platform
North Charleston, South Carolina

To Whit Webster and Cal Webster, my two sons, who have taught me so much about life and love. Walt Sutton was right when he said Children are the great humanizing experience.

And to Dr. Debra Doud whose love has taught me synchronicity is real and affirmations work. She is the lover, friend, partner and confidant whom I've longed for, for so many years.

TABLE OF CONTENTS

INTRODUCTION

While writing this book I often reflected on my junior year at Palm Springs High School, standing in front of the class reading from *Julius Caesar* and hating every moment. I was in my mid-forties when I was diagnosed with dyslexia and then it dawned on me why I hated English class. Reading and writing were always difficult. During the same evaluation that brought dyslexia to my attention I was tested for creativity and found I was in the upper 98% of adults my age. But even then, I still didn't feel comfortable with my writing skills.

My dyslexia would keep me from taking assignments that required me to write on a flip chart in front of a room of strangers. It was okay if they knew me and my strengths, but otherwise my disability caused me great angst. Then in my late fifties I realized that I had strengths that were very helpful to others and I was allowing these fears and weaknesses to hold me back from expressing my gifts.

Someone once said *Build up your weaknesses until they become your strong points.* This is one of the worst pieces of advice I've ever heard. Think of all the wasted effort and frustration for a great sumo wrestler trying to be a ballet star. What I believe is *Work so hard on your strengths that your weaknesses become irrelevant.* Don't let your weaknesses define you.

Fast forward to 1999 in Irvine California at the Vistage (then TEC) annual Chair Conference. Looking at the agenda I read *11:00 a.m. David Whyte,*

Poet. My good friend Dr. Larry King and I always played basketball at the conferences during lunch and I thought, *Great we can leave at eleven and get in an extra hour of basketball.* But Larry insisted we attend. *We'll sit in the back of the room. If we don't like it we'll leave early.*

That one-hour speech by David changed my life and opened a whole new world of creativity through writing and poetry. A few years later I wrote the following poem. And that is how this book began.

I Salute David Whyte

When the student is ready the teacher appears
When the student is ready the teacher appears
Lost sad tired unhappy
I arrived

Wanting a spiritual injection
Needing an inspiring experience
Convinced a run on the hardwood with Dr. King was the tonic I
    needed

The good Doctor insisted
We'll sit in the back and go play ball if we get bored
I asked *What does an Irish poet have for me?*

I need intensity
I need diversion
I need competition
I need to sweat
I need my old friend's wisdom

I sat in the back with 300 or more
I wanted to hit the door
The grinding introduction
I could be driving the lane

Then as if a wave from the nearby cold Pacific washed over me
I was awakened and transfixed
By the Irish poet

He awakened my soul as if it had been asleep forever
He spoke to my pain
My selfishness
My aloneness
My mindless obsession with money and power
My feeling of living a life of lost opportunity
He shared his passion for a life of meaning

Not being lost in the woods
And meeting myself at my own door
He opened my eyes and opened my soul
No need to drive the lane
I'm out of pain

Each of us is unique and moved by different things. For you it might be great artwork by Van Gogh or a symphony by Tchaikovsky or a soulful song by Adele, or maybe the *Holstee Manifesto*. Part of tapping into our inner passion is finding those things that touch our soul. Writing poetry has opened a part of me that I didn't know existed. My hope is that this book will open a similar door for you.

Footnote

The first two lines of the last stanza of the poem refer to two poems David Whyte recited at the meeting: *Lost* by David Wagoner and *Love After Love* By Derek Walcott

One

THE JOURNEY INWARD

What has been so fascinating is how much writing and poetry have taught me. While writing I've been surprised to see the words that flow onto the page. As an example, late at night during a time when I was very conflicted in my personal life, I wrote the following journal entry. Five days later I had a heart attack.

Poem of Discovery

I'm pissed, I'm angry, I'm disappointed
How did I get here?!!!
What the hell do I want?
What the hell do I do?
Life is so good and yet so bad!!!

If my life is the sum total of all my thoughts and actions
I have created an inedible stew of my life

WHAT THE FUCK!!!
WHAT THE FUCK!!!

Don't I have something more intelligent to say?!!!
Can't I be more articulate?!!!

Where do I start?
Age 62.75 and I'm here?!

I'm not stuck
I'm human
I'm spiritual
I'm growing

It is not the end
It is the rest of now

I'm longing
I'm longing

For a friend who is my lover, confidant, partner
How do I want to live the rest of my life?

My heart attack was a watershed event. Two days later while still in the hospital my heart stopped requiring three shocks from a defibrillator to bring me back. If I had not been in the hospital when that happened I wouldn't be writing this. My first thought after the heart attack was *I must have more to do.*

At the time of my heart attack my focus was on work, family, sports and giving back to the community. I wanted to continue to keep the company growing and get back to basketball and tennis. I wanted to get healthy, and live a long time so I could see my sons have families. When I was in cardiac re-hab walking on the treadmill, the nurses kept saying *Slow down!* But I wanted to get back to full strength as fast as I could.

Then late one afternoon while gradually re-engaging in work I was going through some papers on my desk and found my journal. I had forgotten the journal entry above. It was a loud message of the need to deal with the pain it revealed. What I also discovered was that many of my journal entries over the years were more poetic than I realized. Journaling was opening a door to my soul and allowing the music to escape and be heard. Learning how the subconscious speaks through writing led me to a deeper level of self-awareness.

Becoming fully present is not easy in today's society. With the pressure to stay plugged in via the ubiquitous technological umbilical cord twenty-four hours a day, we create little space for reflection and soulful work. So much of our life is just momentum and we often go zombie-like from day to day without asking *Is this what I want my life to be about?* Taking time to journal, talking at a deep level with wise friends or taking a personal retreat away from the routines of life gives an opportunity to ask ourselves *Why am I here? Is this the most important thing I can be doing now? What feeds my soul? What am I pretending not to know right now?* You might start the process by asking the open-ended question *What are the things I need to address in my life to feel it has meaning?* The quality of your questions will affect the path they take you down. Having the right answer to the wrong question is of no value. The wrong question might look like *Why am I unhappy in my job?* The right question might be *What makes me happy?* Or *What is my life's purpose and am I living a life congruent with that purpose?* The nature of the question should be focused on the underlying cause or source of the problem not the problem itself. Invest time to get away from the routine and noise of daily life and reflect. Then you'll start on a journey of a richer more soulful life.

An unexamined life is not worth living.
An unlived life is not worth examining.
Socrates

The first step is to take the first step. Since I started this journey I've been amazed by all the good fortune that has been bestowed upon me by just starting. People with good ideas and support have shown up to help me when I needed them. This is a poem I wrote at David Whyte's Invitas program on Whidbey Island, which has come true for me.

Act Now

When I act! The Universe provides me with all I need
When I act! Doors open, help arrives
When I act! The unknown will become known

The poem's message to me was to get going and write this book. ACT NOW!!

Two

The Power Of Self Discovery
Through Writing

The power of writing as a means to reflect and learn is available to all. Who would have thought that I would expand my world through writing?

I grew up unaware that I had dyslexia. If I hadn't dated English majors and had understanding professors in college I never would have graduated. My first job out of college was managing a department in a retail store. Managing ten people didn't require writing, just verbal communication. When I was told I was being promoted to the world headquarters in a marketing job, it never occurred to me that part of the job was communicating with thousands of people through the written word. My first few writing assignments didn't go well. My boss called me in and asked if I knew how to write. He took me under his wing and gave me several helpful hints that made a big difference. He said write as if you are having a conversation with the reader and use bullet points to make it easy to read and understand. Repetition and trial and error were worthy teachers and my writing became acceptable but never a strength. I'm thankful for my administrative assistants who kept the spelling and punctuation errors to a minimum.

Despite the eventual diagnosis of dyslexia, my dislike for writing continued until recently as I learned how valuable the process is when unencumbered by spelling and punctuation. By letting go of my fear of being judged stupid by my peers, I was at last freed to do what has become my newfound passion.

Late at night while reflecting and journaling about the day and where my life was headed, the words on the paper began to tell a story. While some of the thoughts were familiar many of the words helped me see things through a different lens and brought thoughts to the surface I had ignored or didn't realize existed. The more late night inspiration, the more comfortable I became and the more I looked forward to the reflection time. David Whyte's speech helped me understand the power of conversation and the way to start writing poetry or journaling when blocked. Just say *I want to write about....* This exercise showed me the power that poetry has to uncover and express my deepest feelings. By opening this door to your mind you will see things you are avoiding or that you are unaware of.

You have to create space in your life to write. A good way to get started is the twenty-minute flow exercise. Set an alarm for twenty uninterrupted minutes, put your pen on the page, and just start writing and don't stop until the alarm goes off. Then go back and read it. After a few days, reread it again. Over time you will have discovered themes, ideas and maybe fears that you have been avoiding.

A Poet's Soul

Isn't it interesting how poetry exposes a little of us every time we write
A journey of
Self-discovery
Self-deception
Self-disclosure

We share a little of our soul each time we *put it out there*
We discover a little more of who we are

Sometimes it seems it would be easier to hide
Not write
Not explore

But Socrates was right
An unexamined life is not worth living

Each poem is a pathway to self-examination
And eliminates one more place to hide from self

Listen To Your Words

Put into words how you feel

Write what needs to be written

What needs to be examined

Open your mind and put all your thoughts onto the page

Strike through those that hold you back

Open your soul to what feeds you

Feast on the words that give you courage to go on

Open your mind to your heart

Learn from your words

Let them guide you and comfort you through life

Life is A Poem

Life is a poem written on a blank page
Life is a poem that reflects each stage
Life is a poem that changes with age
Sometimes it feels like the words of a sage
Sometimes it reflects frustration or rage
Sometimes I wish I had a new page

Passion

Passion is the energy
That brings the soul alive

Passion gives energy to love
Passion gives energy to art
Passion gives energy to evolve

Passion bonds lovers
Passion bonds nations
Passion bonds seekers

Passion is what makes life worth living
A life without passion is a life without soul

I Gave You The Power

My phone rang
My heart sang
Then I see it is not you
I don't know what to do
My heart sinks
My life stinks
I keep working to get you off my mind
I realize I gave all my power to you
I'm taking it back

I'm Not My Balance Sheet

I'm not numbers on a page waiting to be totaled

Compared
Analyzed
Balanced
Monetized
To determine my value

I'm a human being whose net worth isn't measured in dollars
I'm a human being whose net worth is measured in friends

Whose net worth is measured
By love given
By love expressed
By love received

Total me up in dollars and all you have is a number and a list of stuff
Total me up in love and friendships and it will equal a rich life

Turning Point

When the day dawns and hope abounds
There is a point when everything changes
This is the turning point

When our optimism can no longer mask the reality of the day
When the pain of staying is greater than the pain of leaving
Each of us has a turning point

It may be a relationship
It may be a job
It may be a friend

There will come a time when you need to stop going in the wrong direction
Meeting that turning point

With the knowledge that it will be better on the other side
Takes courage

We seldom see how good life will be
But it can't be without taking the turning point

Three

LETTING GO OF THE PAST

Two years after I heard David Whyte for the first time, my friend and colleague Charlie Davis urged me to travel to the Hudson River to an isolated old convent to hear David again. I resisted because of all the things that needed to be done. Although I had been inspired by David, I wasn't sure if another retreat was worth the time and money.

After my first experience, I had been moved by his work but had done little to follow up other than reading his book, *The Heart Aroused.* I was busy with work and again not giving myself time for reflection.

A voice in my head said *Chip, you need to go.* And so there I was, sitting with my friend Charlie and his wife Jo, listening to David speak of how many of us drag the past around in a bag stuffed with past regrets. And as time goes on the sack of *stuff* gets bigger and bigger and the list longer and longer. As he spoke a picture formed in my mind of me, dragging this growing bag of the past like a tired old man with it getting caught in car and elevator doors as I trudged through life being held back by the past.

When we spend so much time and energy on trying to have a better past, we'll never have the bright future we are capable of.

For me the first step of this journey was to let go of the past.

Let Go

LET GO LET GO

Of all you don't want

GRAB ON GRAB ON

To what feeds your soul

LET'S GO LET'S GO

And live life with passion

I'm Tired of Hiding

I'm tired of hiding
Where it is safe

There is no passion in safe
There is no growth in safe

I'm tired of hiding
Where it is safe

Time to go and crash against myself
Time to go and crash into the barriers I've created

To break through into the vulnerable space of
Authenticity and Grace

Chip Webster

Nothing is Lost

Deep pain of loss
Of a dream
Of a love
Of a friend

The world is closing in
On my joy
On my heart
On my mind

I feel the sapping
Of my hope
Of my energy
Of my drive

I feel afraid and alone
Then I settle in and know

The Universe can't get it wrong

I feel the peace
About my dream
About my love
About my joy

I am not lost
I am alive

Alone

I lie on a cold lonely hotel room bed at 4 am
I can't sleep
I've been here a thousand times

I hear the whine of the truck tires on the interstate
Wondering where they are headed
And wondering where I'm headed

Fear of loneliness has stopped me from doing
What I need to do

No longer

I have been warmed by the knowledge
That I can't get it wrong
I no longer fear being alone

Time to get up and on the road
I will not be alone again
As long as I am on the road to my next adventure

Finding Now

I feel the tug of the past
I feel the pull of tomorrow
As I try to find Now

The past holds me back
As if it is all I'll ever have
The future is vague and alluring

I keep trying to get to Now
Because it is all I have

When I find the present
I feel the universe's gift to me

I feel the wind on my face
I feel the touch of a child's hand
I feel the power of Now

It is all that is real
It is all that I have

Beginnings

This is not the end it is the beginning
This is not the end it is the beginning

Open the door to your new life
Open the door to your new life

Go make a difference
Go share your wisdom
Go grow your passion
Go make love with life

Go have a conversation with the world
This is not the end it is the beginning

We'll See

Surrender to the mystery
Surrender to the unknown

So much of knowing is
A mirage for the ego

So much of life is
A beautiful surprise

Let go
And let life unfold

Let go
Of ego's need to know

We'll see where life goes

The Last Day of Basketball

Up early ready to run
Got to the gym
It was going to be fun

Up and down the court we ran
We won the last one

Post-game breakfast
We looked forward to next week

Then the news – your body is done
You are at great risk when you run

But it's so much fun
The camaraderie the energy
It makes me feel young

All true but you're done

Ok my body hurts and I can't turn my neck
One more wrong hit and you'll be beyond done

Ok I guess I'm done
Goodbye boys
Goodbye men

Youth is gone
I move on

Endings

The chilling sleet scratches at the window
The hazy glow of the streetlight reflects off the waiting cab's dull yellow paint

The scent of her sweet perfume clings to my body
The memory of her body pressed to mine draws me back to bed
But it has all been said
There is no going back

I dress while watching her fitful sleep
Is she really asleep or wanting to avoid the ending
As I see the curve of her body under the blanket
I remember the passion that brought us together

I tiptoe from her room and from her life
Not wanting to wake her
We'd said it all
Felt it all

As I slid onto the cold vinyl seat and said *LaGuardia* to the driver
I glanced up to the dark window with the pain of loss

What could have been
Got lost in what was

The empty streets of a sleeping New York reflect the empty feeling in my gut
Another ending

The bright lights of LaGuardia bring me back to the now
and a place no longer of endings
But of another beginning

Repack Your Bags

We all have baggage
Filled with our past

Some beat up and ripped
Some with tags from exotic places we've been
Some looking brand new -- never been out of the attic

All full of our past

Usually filled with loss
What we did wrong
Negative words from uncaring and unknowing souls

We drag our baggage after us
Wishing for a better future
But unwilling to let go of the past

Open it up
Open it up

Toss out the bad report cards
Toss out the broken heart

The failed relationship
The loss of a loved one
The negative words that have rung in your ears for 40 years

Your father's prediction *You'll never amount to anything*

Toss them all out

Repack them with your dreams
Repack them with your unique gifts
Repack them with your passion

Load them on a plane to your favorite destination

And go fly

Four

The Passion Of Love

Of all the passions that we have in life, few if any can rival the passion of love. Wars have been fought, fortunes made and lost because of the passion of love. No matter how old we are, no matter the gender, passion is a compelling drug.

The relationship between lovers is the most electric in the human experience both positively and negatively. I was once told that the opposite of love is not hate, it's indifference. In a loving relationship, there is no indifference, unless the relationship is dead. After 33 years raising two wonderful sons my former wife and I came to a point when it was best for us to go our separate ways. It wasn't obvious to me the negative impact the relationship was having on me until late that night I wrote the "Poem of Discovery" referred to in the introduction, and as noted earlier, five days later I had my heart attack. I realized that staying in the relationship wasn't doing her any favors and I was killing myself slowly. It took several years of agonizing to finally leave my marriage. The exercise of writing that I had learned to cherish helped me see more clearly what needed to happen.

For me writing is a way to put feelings on a page and see the situation through a clearer lens, not fogged by the moment, and allows the subconscious to be tapped. Gaining clarity in the love-obsessed state of mind is not easy. My poems are mainly autobiographical. As in the poem "Endings" they start out feeling like fiction but turn out to be premonitions. They represent the process I've used to make sense of a situation, and to understand the passion that was coursing through my mind and body. These poems have been a vehicle to help me better understand love, passion and the spell they can put me under.

First Night

Streets still wet from a hard rain
I drive east with the soft fragrance of her on my clothes
I reflect on our five minutes of just holding each other

The dinner conversation
Her deep probing questions
Her beautiful smile
The way she cocks her head and leans into her questions

Her need to cautiously and wisely move forward
Her wisdom and brilliance is compelling

As I hear her pounding heart in my head
Remember the feel of her warm body pressed to mine
I am content

What can this become
Can we grow and create the bliss we both seek

Only time can tell

The Drug of Love

Two lovers kiss for the first time
Hair gone gray
Joints aching
Years gone by
Sixty
Seventy
Eighty
The chemistry clicks
The pheromones released
And we're eighteen again
Two lovers kiss for the first time
And two hearts come alive

Match.com

Match.com
Eharmony.com
OkCupid.com

All places lonely hearts go
All places fantasies grow
All places where dreams can be dashed on the rocks of reality

After all the *tell me about yourself*
After all the *let's have coffee*
After all the *let's have dinner*

The days
The nights
The weekends

How do I know you are the one
How do I know I'm not in denial
How do I know it will work

I don't know
I have to trust my gut
I have to risk being hurt

Then I can let go and feel your love without fear
Then I can let go and feel your love as it is
Then I can let go and just be loved

Chip Webster

The Dry Riverbed of Love

I walk alone across the harsh desert of unfulfilled love
Searching for the special one that quenches my thirst

I come to a sun-bleached river bed filled with beautiful interesting stones
As I gaze across the stones I see each as a potential lover
It is up to me to turn them over to discover my one lover

I walk into the field of sun drenched stones and start turning them over

    Too needy
    Too narcissistic
    Too flighty

Then I turn over your stone
And your face appears and lures me into the cool damp sand
Giving me the clue it just might be you
It draws me to dig deeper into who you are

Under your resting place after digging deeply into your soul
I find a cool underground stream that quenches my thirst
And we drink together from the sweet water of love

Bliss

As the sun rises
After a long stormy night on the sea of life
The clouds thinning as the sun's rays warm my body
I feel the bliss of being alive

I feel your gentle breath on my neck and I feel content
I feel the warmth of your love surrounding me like an ocean
After years of darkness and aloneness
I feel the bliss of being alive

Tangled Up In You

Together in our special space
Detached from the world
I'm tangled up in you

In your arms in our place of passion
Separated from all the world's troubles
I'm tangled up in you

Together focused on you
What's outside doesn't matter
When I'm tangled up in you

Moonbeams

My moon setting in the west is rising in your east

Know that on your moonbeams my love notes travel

Oh my lover knowing that on the same moon we gaze

Brings joy to me tonight

Counting the Days

I've been counting the weeks till I hold you in my arms
I've been counting the days till I hold you in my arms
I've been counting the hours till I hold you in my arms

I've missed your touch
Your scent
Your kisses

I look at your picture
Try to feel you in my mind
But it makes me miss you more

Soon will come the time
When your body will be next to mine

The Thin Thread of Life

We seek a partner in life
We seek a partner in learning
We seek a partner in love

Sometimes they seem impossible to find
Sometimes they seem impossible to feel
Sometimes they seem impossible to fulfill

The thin thread of life leads us to learn
The thin thread of life leads us to live
The thin thread of life leads us to love

The thin thread of life has led me to you

May the thread never be broken
May we nurture it into a golden chain
Of unbroken love

Real Love

After the lust
After the infatuation

If there is anything left
It is real love

A deep long lasting love
Of respect
Of trust
Of a deep commitment to be together

When real love begins
It is the first sign of adult love

A deep commitment begins to grow
To listening
To understanding
To each other

The passion grows to be connected
At a level far beyond lust and infatuation

Five

WE'RE ALL IN THIS TOGETHER...
NOW WHAT DO WE DO?

There are no passengers on spaceship earth. We are all crew.

MARSHALL MCLUHAN

When we understand the reality of Mr. McLuhan's thoughts, then we can come together and take care of our fragile little planet as it spins through space. We can spend less time and energy focused on our differences and more time and energy on how we can make our world better and safer. We are all in this together. Our legacy can be either that we failed to find a common ground and allowed our differences to destroy the earth, or that we came out of our drunken stupor of small tribal rivalries, with no regard for the big picture, and left the world better than we found it for future generations.

We live in a period where the pace of change is ever increasing and our need to make sense of life is becoming more difficult. The shrinking world has made it more difficult to isolate ourselves in a community of likeminded individuals. We must learn to coexist with those who have a different perspective. We are all in this together and we can influence the outcome. If we don't like the direction of our community, our country, or our world we have to take action. We are the only ones who can change the world.

How can we ever get on the same page if we don't sit down and listen to each other and discuss how we are alike instead of focusing on our differences? Whether it be with your family, community, country or fellow citizens of the earth, the conversation is the relationship. My experience tells me that the quality of the conversation is the quality of the relationship.

Many years ago during a time of deep reflection the thought came to me that we are on earth to grow, help others grow and work together to leave it better than we found it. In a way it's like God using earth as a big team building exercise. Many of you have had the experience at your company or community organization where teams are put together to solve problems and overcome obstacles. The objective is to break down barriers and teach us how we are interdependent. Not just for our organization, but for our family, community and our global success. So far we aren't doing so well.

Out beyond the field of wrongdoing
and right doing there is a field.
I'll meet you there.

RUMI

Some people say, *This is God's will,* and unless you agree with them you are an infidel. This implies *In order for me to be right you must be wrong.* Such black-and-white thinking ends conversations, severs relationships and starts conflicts. If we live in a polarized echo chamber with like-minded individuals who affirm our beliefs or fantasy of how life should be, then we are totally out of touch with reality.

There are two things I've observed over and over about humans. There are great disparities between our behavior and the so-called norms. Hypocrisy is the norm in many cultures. Secondly we live on this earth with 7,400,000,000 other people and we expect all 7,399,999,999 to agree with us, based on our family and culture of origin. Really!!!

Doing the same thing over and over and expecting a different result is the first sign of insanity.

ALBERT EINSTEIN

How Has This Been Working For Us

Global warming
Global cooling

Prohibition
Legalized drugs

Social injustice
Corporate greed

Socialist
Communist
Capitalist
Fascist

White Supremacist
Black Muslim

Christian
Jew
Muslim
Buddhist

Like it or not we are all in this together
Our grandparents may have hated each other
And taught me to hate you

How has this been working for us

In The Name of God

Lives lived in fear
Lives lived in war

Lives lived in judgment
Lives lived in separation

Does he or she really want us to play God

Chip Webster

Angels and Friends

Sometimes friends are so much like angels
    it is hard to tell the difference

Each time we reach out and help another
    it makes a difference

Each time a friend lets us lean on them
    it makes a difference

May I be an angel in your life
    and make a difference

Being angels for each other will make
    all the difference

Angels enrich our lives in so many ways
    They listen
    They share
    They challenge

They make us feel loved
and that makes all the difference

Can We Trust You

The President
The Senate
The House
Can we trust you

Can we trust you to

Act in the best interest of us all
Act to uphold the Constitution
Act to sustain our national strength

Do you understand what is at stake
Do you put the nation ahead of your ego
Do you put the nation ahead of your need to be re-elected
Do you put the nation ahead of your personal gain

Can we trust you to

Not pander to a few
Not pander to the lobbyists
Not pander to the wealthy
Not pander to the special interests

Can we trust you to keep us free and equal

The Paradox of Man

When I was the stream, ... When I was every hoof, foot, fin and wing,... no one ever asked me did I have a purpose, no one ever wondered was there anything I might need. For there was nothing I could not love. Meister Eckhart

Jesus said *God is love*
The Muslims say *Islam means peace*
Ah nature so peaceful so ordered so loving

Has anyone noted that the lion eats the lamb to survive
Has anyone noticed the majestic hawk eats the mouse to survive

Man risks life to save cat
Man risks life to save child
Woman gives kidney to save stranger

We can be so irrational with our hate
Hated because we were born black or white or Christian or Jew

OH WHAT CAN WE DO

Can we stop chopping each other's heads off if we disagree
Can we stop the raping
Can we all just get along

As mankind we've come so far and yet we haven't changed at all

Polite societies overrun by hordes
More lambs eaten by lions

At our core we are still in a Darwinian world
The survival of the fittest is still reality
We fight to defend ourselves from those who want us dead

Oh the Paradox

I have felt love from strangers
Given love to strangers
And feared the unknown
The different

The lion will lie with the lamb till it gets hungry
How do we consolidate our human behavioral gains
And defeat our animal tendencies

Oh the Paradox of Man

Who's Right

For me to be right
Do you have to be wrong

It seems so wrong for just one of us to be right
Isn't diversity of thought good

Creative
Expansive

We can't all be right and all be wrong

We can learn from each other
We can create something new

That isn't right or wrong
But good and different

Black and White

It all seems black and white to me

Then I study each element

Each stroke of the brush

Going deeper

Looking deeper

It turns to gray

Going even deeper

I see the complexity of it all

It isn't black and white after all

I Argue Unfairly

I argue unfairly
> I expect you to agree with me

I argue unfairly
> I expect you to see what I see

I argue unfairly
> It goes nowhere

I argue unfairly
> Because I don't listen to you

Speaking Truth

I speak based on what I know now

As now becomes yesterday

As new truth becomes apparent

As old truth becomes obsolete

My truth evolves

Calling All Poets, Writers, Musicians and Artists

We want you!
Western Civilization wants you!
Freedom loving people want you!

You are the creative force that moves our soul
You are the creative force that moves our culture
You are the creative force that moves us to action

New York Paris and Madrid are calling
Our unborn children are calling
The repressed women of the world are calling

We are at a crossroad
A battle between good and evil
A battle between Western Civilization and the Dark Ages

Are we perfect
No
Are we reaping the blood of past mistakes
Yes
Are we willing to defend our way of life

There is a choice to be made
There is a commitment to be made
Western Civilization is at war
With extremists and all they represent

We must rally our fellow lovers of enlightenment
We must not be timid
We must not stumble on Political Correctness

WE ARE AT WAR

We must see it as a war of ideas not nations
We must see it as a war of two world visions
We must see it as a war for the survival of Western Civilization

Sound your trumpets
Write your inspiring words
Paint pictures that call us to act

Six

LEGACY

I was interviewing the CEO of a company to become a member of my Vistage group. It was an in-depth conversation. I asked him to describe his culture. He paused and asked *I've always wanted a culture; how do I get one?* His well-established multi-generational company had been stalling over the past few years. Based on my brief exposure, their culture didn't seem to have any energy. He didn't realize he had a very strong culture, but it was a culture of everyone for themselves. There was no compelling vision to serve the customer or enjoy the success of the team together. It was a culture by default rather than a culture of intention. Over the next few years I followed his demise. We know culture is more powerful than strategy. Culture determines the success of a family, state or country and yes, the world.

So why a discussion of culture in a chapter on Legacy? Legacy is the result of culture over a long period of time. The quality of the culture determines the quality of the legacy. Clarity and intention are the first steps to a successful culture and thus a quality legacy. Knowing first what we want our legacy to be can lead to a more intentional development of our culture.

Many of our election campaigns are reflections of our current culture and sometimes an embarrassment and not the legacy we want to be remembered for. The behavior of many candidates with their disregard for the truth has become the norm. We have the government and culture we deserve, because we allowed it to develop. We haven't been clear, intentional or committed to leaving the world better than we found it.

> *Public business, my son, must always be done by*
> *somebody or other. If wise men decline it, others will*
> *not; if honest men refuse it; others will not.*

JOHN ADAMS

Only we can change the culture of today and thus change the legacy that we will be remembered for. We have to answer *What do we want our great grandchildren to tell their great grandchildren about us?* The first step is to own the answer and commit the time and money to create the change we want.

Great Grandchildren

Grandpa
Tell me about your grandpa

He was an honest hard working man
Working to care for his family

He lived in the golden age
He gave his family all they wanted

He spent his time playing golf
Enjoying the fruits of his labor

He didn't get involved in the community
He didn't bother to vote

He led a good life
He didn't think of the future

Grandpa
Is that why we live in a cave

Think

Turn off your TV

Turn on your mind

Turn off your TV

Turn on your family

Turn off your TV

Turn on your town

Turn off your TV

Turn on your country

Chip Webster

One Man

I want to talk about life
I want to talk about how wonderful and how tragic it can be
It isn't how and what we see
It is what we don't see
And what is

How can we be so kind and so cruel
How can we love one moment and hate the next
We see the love one human has for a child
And yet the next moment
He can kill his fellow man
Because of the color of his skin

It is a mystery to me

Help me see
Help me feel
Help me understand
What one man can do

The Inventors

There are no inventions
Only
Discoveries

Thomas Edison
Worked
And
Worked
Driven by the belief there must be a way to generate light from electricity
He unlocked the principle

Jonas Salk
Worked
And
Worked
Driven by the belief there must be a way to stop polio
He unlocked the principle

Driven by the belief we can cure cancer
A yet unknown seeker
Works
And
Works
To unlock the principle

Driven by the belief we can create social peace
A yet unknown seeker
Works
And
Works
To unlock the principle

Finding the principles that already exist takes
Work
Work
Work
To unlock

We Stand on The Shoulders of Giants

We stand on the shoulders of giants
The ability to fly
The ability to receive a new heart
The ability to travel to the moon

All because we are free
All on the shoulders of giants

Socrates
Galileo
Washington
Churchill
Salk
King
Glenn

Each generation passes their gifts to the next
As they evolve from child to elder to ancestor

It's our time to build strong shoulders
For those that follow
To have strong shoulders to stand on

Moms

They give us life
They give us love
The unconditional kind
Like no other

They suffer through our pain
They rejoice in our joy
They bring us up

Wash your hands
Go to bed
Make your bed
Would you like some cake
I made it just for you
Did you do your homework
What's her name
What is she majoring in
How do you like your new roommate
What an exciting new job
I like her
When is the wedding
What a beautiful son
He reminds me of your father
Can you come for Thanksgiving
I love you

Tears of joy
Tears of pain for a life well lived
She gave us life and love
In the dark hour of her passing we can only say
Thanks I love you Mom

Dad

I never really knew you
Gone at 63
I was 31
We never bonded
You had to be
The Father

Yes Sir
No Sir
Whatever you want
Hard edged solid stone

Your gifts to me
Man of education for others
Integrity
Work ethic
Trustworthy

How not to be a Dad
We never connected
I was never good enough

I took what you didn't give to me and gave it to my sons
Thank you

Old Trees

Old trees majestic and wise
They say trees are the oldest living thing on earth

But old trees must die to make room
For young trees to grow out from the shadows
They need the sun on their limbs to grow

What stories they can tell
Initials of lovers on their trunks
Scarred by battles
Shelter from storms

Each ring tells a story
Drought
Flood
Fire

May I know when it is time to go
So others can grow
Letting their rings multiply

Seven

ENDINGS

Despite all the exercise classes, wonder drugs, magical surgery and fantasy, reality catches up with us: Age. I've often asked, *If you didn't know how old you were, how old would you be?* Even at 70, I've told myself 18.

Now that reality has settled in, basketball and skiing are over. I've decided now (well most of the time) to embrace each of the remaining stages of life, taking time to reflect on what has been learned from many friends, experiences, children and career. Now is the time to savor life, reflect upon it, and learn from it. And it's the time to share life's lessons with those I love and those who care to listen.

The illusion that we will live forever seems to be a universal human condition. The denial of our mortality serves us well until the illusion is exposed. The longer the time we spend in the illusion, the bigger the impact when we are brought up short by reality. I have watched several CEOs who framed their lives in *If I die* terms, leaving their families and businesses in horrible condition. They refused to face the reality that they weren't invincible, and failed to plan for succession. The very business they wanted to continue after their passing, dissolved because it was easier to say *If I die* rather than *When I die*. It was interesting to watch how much energy they put into that illusion and how it kept them from dealing with their business in the best way. In addition, and even more importantly, personal relationships were put on the back burner for *When I have time* that was never realized.

There are many paradoxes in life and this is one of them. All we have is the now, and to not enjoy it is a lost opportunity for a happy life. Not being in the now melts away our passion and makes each day a little less fulfilling. We only have the now to live in. Yet if we fail to plan for the future and take appropriate actions, our loved ones will suffer.

We only get one bite at the apple of life. We can live it fully or in a little box created in our mind with the illusion that our little world is safe. All my experiences tell me the whole game is about being willing to take risks. And, knowing at the end of the day, that life is about the people you took the risk with, to love and to nourish.

Life is A Mosaic

Life is a mosaic
Made of tiles that represent each human interaction
Some bright and beautiful
Some dark and painful
Some large
Some small
Each a moment of my life
When life is fading
As I look back
And see it finished for the first time
It will be a likeness of me

My Gift of Life

It is mine no one else can open it
It is mine no one else can wear it
It is mine and it just fits me
So do I save it for the perfect time to wear it
Or do I use it up and share it
I've been slowly opening it
Getting ready to share it
To use it all up
If I don't use it
It will be lost forever

Old Toes

Discolored
Wrinkled
Old peoples' toes

I used to be repulsed
At the sight of
Old peoples' toes

Today I looked at my feet
And saw
Old peoples' toes

Then I remembered
Dancing
Skiing
Running
With my young toes

Now I see my
Wise old toes

Chip Webster

Not Today

I don't feel great every day

Sometimes I want to say

World

Just go away

I'm staying in bed today

I'll come out and play another day

Just go away

I Saw Death Last Night

I was in a deep sleep
I awoke in my dream to a golden sunset on Lido Beach
The warm sun on my shoulders
reflected the golden sky off the windows of the buildings

As I looked at the end of the day
I looked at the end of my life

A warm gentle glow and a feeling of peace touched my soul
It was the sunset

Glide Path

It's not what I want to think about today
It's not what I want to talk about today

But at this age I'm in my final glide path
In my final decent into the next phase of existence
Whatever it might be

I was thinking of a good friend's birthday
And calling him to ask
How does it feel to be ...

At 12 I wanted to be 13
At 20 I wanted to be 21
At this age I want to be fully alive

Letting the updrafts of love and friendship
Carry me along my glide path

Epilogue

This journey together has come to an end. My hope is that it has been valuable to you as you navigate your own life's journey. David Whyte opened my soul to the power of writing and poetry. These gifts enriched my life by opening my soul.

One of my favorite Whyte poems is "Start Close In". His words ring in my head as this book comes to a close.

> *Start close in,*
> *don't take the second step*
> *or the third,*
> *start with the first*
> *thing*
> *close in,*
> *the step*
> *you don't want to take.*

> Start with
> the ground
> you know,
> the pale ground
> beneath your feet,

your own
way to begin
the conversation.

Start with your own
question,
give up on other
people's questions,
don't let them
smother something
simple.

To hear
another's voice,
follow
your own voice,
wait until
that voice
becomes a
private ear
that can
really listen
to another.

Start right now
take a small step
you can call your own
don't follow
someone else's
heroics, be humble
and focused,

start close in,
don't mistake
that other
for your own.

Start close in,
don't take
the second step
or the third,
start with the first
thing
close in,
the step
you don't want to take.

Printed with permission of the author

When struggling to get started, David's instruction of beginning with the statement *I want to talk about…* inspired this book and the following poem. I answered the question and wrote "The Journey to This Place in Time."

The Journey to This Place in Time

Skinned knees I learned to ride a bike
Bloody nose I learned how to fight

Standing on the boy's side of the gym I wondered how I looked when I danced
After college I met a woman and wondered if I had a chance

Careers established
Families started

I'm supposed to be an adult
I'm supposed to be responsible

Children leave an empty nest
I ask what's next

No longer about work
No longer about responsibility

I don't need permission
I know how it ends

I ask what do I want
I ask what is my legacy

What is in me that still needs to be let out
The passion comes out

My next step is to take the step I don't want to take

About The Author

C hip Webster was born in California and currently resides in St. Petersburg, Florida. He has two grown sons and has a wonderful loving relationship with Deb Doud. He graduated from Drake University and spent much of his career with Vistage, leading CEO think tank forums both as a group Chair and eventually as President of Vistage Florida.   He is a past recipient of the Vistage International Don Cope Memorial Award and co-founded TEC / Vistage *Keepers of the Flame.* Currently he leads the CEO roundtable for Florida Funders, an early stage funding source for start-up companies, as well as counseling CEO's. In his free time he enjoys family, boating, travel and poetry.

About The Artist

Terry Brett, a native of St Petersburg, comes from a family of artists. His grandmother was an award-winning Illinois painter and his mother an accomplished portrait artist. Terry is the former chairman of the Morean Arts Center in St. Petersburg and is represented by Red Herring Gallery in Tampa, and Leslie Curran Galley in St. Petersburg

Acknowledgements

There are so many wonderful people who have enriched my life. It would take a book the size of the Webster's Unabridged Dictionary to list them all. The first is Deb whose support and encouragement kept me going when I wondered if it was worth the time and effort. Not only did she give me moral support, she labored beside me to be sure my spelling, punctuation and syntax were correct. Secondly, Dr. Heather Sellers, my good friend and writing coach who encouraged me to publish this book. And Dr. W. Craig Gilliam who nudged me along and kept asking *When are you going to press?*

Others whose friendship and encouragement have kept me going: My high school friends especially Mick Johnston, Ron Boggs, Bob Watt and Tom Boese. Also, my Vistage community Members and Chairs, and especially the Keepers of the Flame Climbing Team: Glenn Waring, Dennis Kleper, Doug Bouey, Peter Buchanan and Rick Marten. A special thanks to Peter Meinke the Poet Laureate of Florida and Helen Wallace the Poet Laureate of St. Petersburg who took time to encourage a struggling not-so-young poet. And my guardian angels, Richard Gilbert and Julie Gammack.

There are many more but I want to especially thank Terry Brett for his art, wisdom and friendship.

And last but not least, Tina Sutter who is a true editing genius.

Alphabetical Index of Poem Titles

INDEX OF FIRST LINES

Made in the USA
Middletown, DE
28 August 2017